The Crack in Everything

Pitt Poetry Series

The Crack in Everything

Alicia Suskin Ostriker

University of Pittsburgh Press

Published by the University of Pittsburgh Press,
Pittsburgh, Pa. 15260

Copyright © 1996, Alicia Suskin Ostriker

Manufactured in the United States of America

Printed on acid-free paper

Library of Congress Cataloging-in-Publication data and
acknowledgments will be found at the end of this book.

A CIP catalog record for this book is available from the
British Library.
Eurospan, London

*The publication of this book is supported by
grants from the National Endowment for the Arts
in Washington, D.C., a Federal agency,
and the Pennsylvania Council on the Arts.*

There is a crack, a crack in everything
That's how the light gets in

—Leonard Cohen

Contents

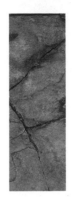

I

The Dogs at Live Oak Beach, Santa Cruz

As if there could be a world
Of absolute innocence
In which we forget ourselves

The owners throw sticks
And half-bald tennis balls
Toward the surf
And the happy dogs leap after them
As if catapulted—

Black dogs, tan dogs,
Tubes of glorious muscle—

Pursuing pleasure
More than obedience
They race, skid to a halt in the wet sand,
Sometimes they'll plunge straight into
The foaming breakers

Like diving birds, letting the green turbulence
Toss them, until they snap and sink

Teeth into floating wood
Then bound back to their owners
Shining wet, with passionate speed
For nothing,
For absolutely nothing but joy.

Boil

Boil over—it's what the nerves do,
Watch them seethe when stimulated,

Murmurs the man at the stove
To the one at the fridge—

Watch that electric impulse that finally makes them
Fume and fizz at either

Frayed end. If you could grasp a bundle
Of nerves in your fist like a jumper cable, and sense that

Python's writhe, or a garden hose when the pressure's
High and it wilfully weaves about

Trying its best to get away from you—
You'd see how nothing is passive,

We're all—I mean from our elephant sun, ejaculant
Great-grandfather, cascading down

To weightless
Unstoppable neutrinos

Leaving their silvery trace
In vacuum chambers, in

Effervescent lines, twisted
Madly in our madhouse jackets,

Rules, laws, which we are seething to break
Though to rupture them might be of course to die,

Or, *possibly,*
To change:

Boil, it's what water
And everything else teaches.

Marie at Tea

You remember the extremes
Wittgenstein says
There is no such thing as ordinary
Experience

My heart aches, literally, and a drowsy
So I wonder if I will die soon
Sometimes I am so tired
I want to

You remember the extremes
I remember when his father died
We took the train into London
Sat in his childhood
And boyhood parlor
Listened to a Joan Baez record
That we always listened to
And when she began singing
"The Great Silkie," a tragic
Scottish folk song about fathers
And sons, he threw
His head in my lap and sobbed, I
Never saw him weep again although
I have sobbed and yowled countless times
On his chest his lap his shoulder
I remember when I gave birth
The first time, thirty-six hours in labor
While he was sitting in the labor room
Trying to help me breathe
Through my contractions
Then in a corner reading an
Obstetrics textbook where
Normal childbirth occupied
Fifty pages and possible complications
Five hundred pages
It frightened him so terribly he wanted
To tell the obstetrician if he had a choice
To let the baby go and save his wife

I have always felt
This to be touching
I remember the lunch in the Red Lion
When in tears I begged him
To stop fooling around with the au pair girl
And to my astonishment
He refused. You remember
The extreme things
Not the normal
Uneventful moments
Years decades
Food sex
Screams laughter
Betrayal conciliation
A day at the races
A night at the opera
Everything slightly cracked
Then afterward you say:
We're married this long
Because we are both too stubborn
To admit we made a mistake,
Which is a good line
And a workable disguise

The truth is that you do not know the truth

The kernel of death
Life wraps itself around
Like chamois cloth
Around a diamond

Ice
Cold at the center
Precious no doubt because
Inhumanly old, that
Is my idea of
Love, of marriage, the
Extreme

Alice Before Her Widowhood

I called him fool, she said
It just slipped out
She pulled the laundry out of the dryer
There are some things a woman shouldn't
Ought to say to a man
She sprayed starch on the sheets and pressed them
After they brought him home Friday
And the doctor said to take him to emergency
And this right now after his second
Heart attack
Hypertension, she said
Account of the blood pressure
I told him he shouldn't do this construction work
He said the money being so good, he got to
Says how that doctor last time told him
He could go back to work—
After that second heart attack?
I don't think that doctor cares about
My husband's health
He talk Spanish, that doctor, it mostly Spanish
People in that office
And I said money is less important than your
Health, you fool
It just slipped out like that
I saw his face was hurt
She folded up the sheets
I called him fool.

Revolution as Desire

I would eat these features, eat
the last three or four thousand years, every hair.

—Li-Young Lee

Imagine yourself in the water
When something collects itself,
Drags itself forward and
Clambers upward, the way a Chinese acrobat
In mid-act swiftly mounts a ladder that rests
Upon void, and the moment before
It breaks
You might
From that crest discern numberless smaller waves tossing
Their whitecaps restlessly
To a gray horizon flung like a performer's cape
While before you there would lie the shore—
A hill of sand, trees waving at you
Like peasants waving at passengers
In a train passing their village,
And there is a line of low pastel buildings,
And salt glittering in the windless air—
All astonishingly stationary
As you swim toward it
With such joy,
Such a lovesick roar.

Surfer Days

Those were strange days, when we were kids
Says the bartender
I remember this one kid I met
Doing roadwork down at Huntington Beach
Told me he used to work for some drug dealer
Like the guy was thirty-five and bald
The way I'm getting myself
And Mikey was this cute blond surfer
Eighteen and irresistible, so his
Job was to pick up girls on the beach
Bring them to his boss
If it didn't go right and the girl got away
His boss would beat him up
Knock him down the stairs
That was why he was pouring tar
With a mashed eye
Saving up money for a knucklehead
Harley-Davidson
Says the bartender ruefully
A combination of tough kid and innocent
He wanted to get to Oakland and be a Hell's Angel
And when he got the bike
And got to Oakland
It took forty-eight hours for his bike
And leather jacket to be stolen
And he was back at Huntington Beach—
Didn't know just what to do, finally
Got hold of some bad drugs
Gone like a flash
Strange days.

Migrant

Desire comes up in us
Like the morning sun
Over the Great Central Valley

Perfectly dry and stark
Diagonal rays gilding the fields
And the insects waking in them

The sun sheds a pink light
On the adobe streets—
On the dust—

Not yet aroused
We breathe with ravishment
The cool, blue, untainted inland air

We are already sweating
As we tramp from our trailers
Toward ripeness a mile off

Facing the anger of the sun
The light sound of a motor approaching
And receding is still pleasant

So few people as yet
Getting into their cars and going to work
Blackbirds are audible, we feel like men

Until the moment we bend
Over the stalks, and there it is—
Pain swaggers up

With its hot knives,
Its rotten burlap sacks,
Like changing a channel

To a show that has always been playing.

The Boys, the Broom Handle, the Retarded Girl

Who was asking for it—
Everyone can see
Even today in the formal courtroom,
Beneath the coarse flag draped
Across the wall like something on a stage,
Which reminds her of the agony of school
But also of a dress they let her wear
To a parade one time,
Anyone can tell
She's asking, she's pleading
For it, as we all
Plead—
Chews on a wisp of hair,
Holds down the knee
That tries to creep under her chin,
Picks at a flake of skin, anxious
And eager to please this scowling man
And the rest of them, if she only can—
Replies *I cared for them, they were my friends*

It is she of whom these boys
Said, afterward, *Wow, what a sicko,*
It is she of whom they boasted
As we all boast

Now and again, because we need,
Don't we, to feel
Worthwhile—
As without thinking we might touch for luck
That flag they've hung there, though we'd all avoid
Touching the girl.

In Our Time: A Poem to Aphrodite

Breathing Times Square air
I come off the streets
Between the cars and shills
Enter the terminal where you stagger and snarl
Notice the mucus on your jacket sleeve
The wine, I can't believe it's you, I see
You shudder when the cops come by
I see you prepare your defiance
I say no need, I've been looking for you
Crazy lady, please don't be so bitter
You can stay in my house
Wrapped in your cape of rusty razor blades
You can smash my furniture
Get pissing drunk and break the bottles
Show me your scars
Where they knifed you, the tired lines like zippers,
Sweetheart, the bruise
Marigolds where they punched you out—
Curse me if you want to.
Tomorrow noon the two of us, lady,
Could sit across the table
Hung over, in our bathrobes.
I'd skip work.
I'd make espresso and slice oranges.
I'd watch your eyes that learned bewilderment
When all you loved
Stopped meeting your free, limitless gaze.

Triptych

Tragedy, ecstasy, doom.
—Mark Rothko

Plunging his arms through stormy blue,
Slime green, undulant purple-black,
To dredge the sorrow from a place
So near the ocean floor, so
Bleak, so sympathetic, he
Can rest inside it
Like a sailor's hammock,

Hearing the throb of engines,
Less a sound than a slow
Vibration of his breastbone,
Long, agate waves
Like tribal brothers walking in
Feathers from the moon, moodily slapping
The barnacled hull of the ship,

He turns his blanketed body
Over again, lifting to sleep, and travels
Forward through jade water and starlight.
The drowned tumble
Endlessly in their bags,
Wind blows ceaselessly
Eastward above the surface,

Remote from any earth where buildings stand.

Walker Art Center, Minneapolis

At the Van Gogh Museum

for Rebecca, Eve, and Gabriel

No, we say—it wouldn't have looked like that
To us—but it did look like that
To Vincent Van Gogh, we admit
And when we look at it,
A whole street painted yellow
From the wide pear-colored gutter
In sketchy curly brushstrokes, like peelings,
To the sidewalks and buildings
With their pinkish awnings
And potato or apricot shuttered windows,
We see thick different yellows,
Squash and butter to clear
Citron, then when we keep
Looking we see it isn't the afternoon
Light—which wouldn't have looked like that
Ever—there are no shadows, no
Shadows in the painting! We see it's that
For him a yellow light
Source came from within,
Welled from within everything,
And was pressing up, up
Through the willing surfaces.

We see the yellowest is Vincent's house
On the corner, the one
Painted with the purest
Most childlike passion,
We see its windowpanes
Black, smack
In the center of the canvas
Even blacker than the navy sky.

> *Vincent's House in Arles,*
> Riksmuseum Vincent Van Gogh, Amsterdam

Nude Descending

Like a bowerbird trailing a beakful of weeds
Like prize ribbons for the very best

The lover, producer
Of another's pleasure

He whom her swollen lips await
Might wing through any day of the decade

A form of health insurance
For which it is never too late

Titanic, silver brush
Hindenburg, of exploding cigars a climax

The watery below, the fiery above
Ashes of print between—pigment between

If the crippled woman were to descend
From her bed, her fortress beyond midnight

Downstairs (*nude/staircase*) to the kitchen
Naked to sit at the table (*writing/thinking*)

She might hear the washer spin like a full orchestra
Complete a cycle like a train crash

Before the fiend would stare through the window
Step smoothly into the kitchen, stop some clocks.

Envy shapes a fig tree in one's breast,
That is bluntly to say a cancer,

That is to say
In a mind, a fertile windy field. A murdered child.

Well then, fear, primarily of falling.
Ebony surf toils on the beach, a glaze

At the same moment I am (*from a cliff*) falling
The kitchen fiend removes his Dior tie

Places his hand over the woman's
And softly says: I am the lover.

Now if the crippled woman began to dance
To pirouette, to rumba

Growling for her child
Her burning page, the devil would be shamed

*(Materialism is not for everyone/Religion is
the extension of politics by other means)*

Would disembody like a wicked smoke
Back to the status of myth

Away he'd streak, blue, into the—
O faun, we would finally call, farewell

O faun, we would faintly faintly call
O faun, we would, we would fondly—

She does not dance. She does not wish
To produce another's pleasure.

They have torn her apart
Into beige rectangles.

The Studio (Homage to Alice Neel)

An oily rag at her feet in the warehouse of scents
Releases essence of pine. A steampipe knocks.
A radio urges the purchase of Philip Morris cigarettes,
Ford motor cars, Saks quality slipcovers.
Welcome to America, Grand Central Station,
Crossroads of a nation. There is no heaven and no hell,

You got to understand, this existence is it,
I blame nobody, I just paint, paint is thicker than water,
Blood, or dollars. My friends and neighbors are made
Of paint, would you believe it, paintslabs and brushstrokes
Right down to the kishkes, as my grandfather would say.
Like bandaged Andy, not smart enough to duck.

Palette knife jabs, carnation, ochre, viridian.
Look at them. And look at me, I'm like Rembrandt,
Poor, omnivorous, and made of pity. Made of love.
Like José on the couch with nostrils like Dante's inferno.
The thing about life in the bughouse, says Alice Neel,
Is it's better than killing yourself. And you get some rest.

Insane asylum, bughouse, madhouse, loony bin,
Snake pit, it's like the Eskimo words for snow.
I never appreciated the nuances though.
After a while the life is only boring.
The food condenses to pudding.
The beds were cold oatmeal in the first place.

The unconscious cruelties of the staff cease to amuse you.
And when you find yourself secretly peeking
Through the window bars at menstrual red sunsets,
You decide you cannot tolerate the other loonies another day.
So you behave sanely and leave. Bye-bye!
And you're back in the basement studio.

Appearance and Reality

in memory of May Swenson

Amphibian, crustacean? The nooked neck
Seems always in process of peering

Hesitantly out, or rapidly withdrawing,
Pulling its loose pleats tight again

Back in its turtle shell. It's like a hand
Puppet returned to its lacquered box,

Or a ferocious child imprisoned in
Shyness, but what if we picture

That same child, some long-ago August
In her Utah backyard examining a turtle

That feigns nonentity itself? Tapping it
Where it lies in the pool of her pinafore

With a fingernail to hear the tick,
She has to chuckle. She admires the dish shape,

Checks its polished markings, turns it over
To look at the tough olive underside,

Peers for the claws, the scratchy nails, and then
She wants to see its pursy face.

Shyness pink as the inside of a mouth,
A mouth maybe with many sharpened teeth

And black sandpaper tongue, rough like a cat's,
Worth waiting for. But when the beast emerges,

Not interested in her, it begins instantly
To row away, off her pink cotton

Lap and across the dandelioned lawn,
Headed beyond the painted fence and sunlit

Sidewalk, and makes its escape underneath
The shadow of the blue Nash at the curb.

Quite gone, it leaves her the memory
Of weight and scurry, of dangled unmapped day.

So the child gets set to travel everywhere,
To take a trip by staying still, to take

The planet in, in fond curiosity—
Can it be true she never went anywhere?

For here she is, her tan face elderly
And infantile at once, mixed like geology,

A pleated map or complicated sphere
Under a cap of ash blond baby-hair

Blunt-cut, and so fine that the least breeze
Can lift up tender wisps of it,

Like bits of chick-fluff or kitten-fur,
She's feigning innocence, and letting wander

A pair of blue and stainless eyes,
Almost unlashed, bright as a baby bird's,

On a stocky body (like a Chinese lady's
In a kitchen) private and unembarrassed,

That curious face keeps cheering itself
By watching stuff. It's friendly. Really a mammal.

Globule

It is like what we imagine knowledge to be.
—Elizabeth Bishop

i

To be transparent, to contain the world,
To be jellyfish, lucent, mobile, membraned,

Boneless behold me, my mica bits
Expensive steel suspended in my substance,

Afloat in floodwater, swinging shoreward,
Ebbing oceanward, clockless among quick fishes—

Striped, spotted,
Speckled, stippled—

Swishing between braincoral cobbles,
Granulated brine, ever in motion.

ii

From plate tinted a shell's hard innerness,
Cerise bleeds, leads chilly dawn.

Sunlight struggles downward through wavelets
Near the sound's warm surface, visible even

From the cliffs of cottages, it pushes relentlessly
Finding us, feeding us, diatoms, sea lace,

Anemones, kelp. Breathing in our beds,
Bright sunlight sustains us, formidable father,

We who are oblivious, maybe immortal,
Then softens, slants, abruptly dips. There's darkness.

Brutally cold, the boom of surf unheard,
Over pocked sand, purely indifferent,

Rock ridges ready to razor tenderness,
Seawater keeps moving forgetfully.

iii
Now on the surface moonlight rests like ice,
And the far sky blinks its pointed messages,

Pointless to me, about matter's beginnings—
Membraneous, shapeless, rocking undersea,

Both a thing contained and container of mystery,
Smoothness inside of smoothness, cold in cold,

Wishing only to be as I am, transparent,
Textured fleck afloat in a wet world.

The Orange Cat

for Vikram Seth

The orange cat on the porch
Regards the tiny bird
Out on the pine tree limb
And yawns without a word.

The morning air is mild,
The tawny hillsides seem
Halfway from sleep to waking;
The cat appears to dream,

Which is of course illusion;
A harsh jay on the hill
Is answered by three quail
Clucks, and a warbler's trill.

The cat who is not hungry
Can listen in repose
To bird calls, with that pleasant
Touch of desire's throes

We feel before a painting
Of nude or odalisque,
The lust without the pain,
Arousal without risk

Of failure, mild *frisson*—
Like drink, and no hangover,
Sex without friction, love
Minus the awkward lover.

The Death of the Poet, Hartford 1955

The world his book, it cunningly condenses
To his lap, where his thumbs can smooth the pages.
He is pleased to concentrate, a final time,
On something interesting: glassy whiteness

Covered with notation that might be music,
Might be a fork scraping porcelain
Where a pastoral scene is painted, whose shepherdesses,
Carrying crooks and wearing big hoop skirts,

Are tending woolly sheep and being tended
In turn by shady oaks. But what happens?
First the characters melt, like too many hoof prints,
Then the pages themselves wad together. All gone, said the child.

All gone, said the bright child, showing his clean plate
Proudly, to please the mother.

Deaf Cities

i

When the angel's instructions finished
The cloud puffed away.
People picked up their spears
Killed each other
Went home and feasted
And had themselves painted.
They had done so before,
Would do so afterward.
What was different
About the good, tart, iron smell of blood?
Now there was awe in it.

ii

Something hit the eardrums like spikes.

The cloud puffed along the sky like a trolley.
A green whiff of reminder, a soupspoon of joy
The people were grateful
Violets, or mossy stones.

iii

The angel kept speaking, its hairlike tones
Combusting from nothingness into existence
A miniature computer-paper scroll
Flipping from heaven
All the way down—
Cities congealed in its circumference—
Deaf cities. Rivers felt attracted.

Harp harp harp.
The angel lifted a voice
Like a furious siren
The loser in a beauty contest
The informant in a bureaucracy
It grew alarming
As metal clangs
And it sang through the desolate fumes
Of the house on fire, bombed by the mayor
Courteously
Clap if you think anyone heard.

Philadelphia, October 1985

Anecdotes Without Flowers: 1919

i

This year he interviewed
An old Japanese farmer's wife who sat
In autumn sun reweaving nets, and said
Of her dead infant daughters
Whom she herself had killed,
Because in poor times one did so,
That she still thought of them
Always. She expected
To go to hell for this but understood
The babies also were in hell
And prayed sincerely to meet their spirits
When she arrived there, wishing
To protect them as best she could.

ii

In the same year the Russian noblewoman—
When Kerensky's troops invaded the house
And demanded to know where the kitchen was,
She could not tell them, for she did not know,
For the dumbwaiter had always lifted
Her food up to her,
For the pockmarked servant had always
Served it to her, bowing and murmuring phrases
Of semi-audible musical French
In a clean white shirt and breeches.
But now he too was missing—
So much was missing.

The Russian Army Goes Into Baku

When the ethnic riots start, and the civilized west
Leans forward to cheer hoarsely—
Such is our dread—

What can it mean to sit in a coffee shop
With my friend B——, the newspaper
And a new book of Rumi in my lap,

Forking my pastry, thinking how maybe
Russia can stop the slaughter of Armenians,
Maybe it can't, tonguing

My cappucino, such hatred in the world,
Even the crusades
Not over yet

*

In the first flush of freedom, Turks kill
Armenians, Rumanians kill Turks,
That's an old story, isn't it, remarked

The man in the bookstore who sold me my *Times*,
With its lead photo a shouting crowd shoving
A line of recruits—sure, old as the hills,

Like the old myth that suffering is virtue,
Like the delusion that misery and oppression
Make the soul generous, when anyone can view

That belt of frozen snakes stretched out across
Europe to central Asia, where parents teach children
The annals of martyrdom, *Never forget*

The wounds of Christ, they say, *No God but Allah,*
So that the dormant rage of nations keeps
Fit for revivification, *Only wait*

Albania, Yugoslavia, Bulgaria, Rumania, Greece,
Germany hissing, the snakes in springtime awakening, what fool
So drowned in euphoria as not to be afraid

Someday this ice age will be over
A thaw will come, it must come
Someday we will punish our enemies

*

To gather in only what you can assimilate—see
What the eye sees
With its own eyes

—Don't read the newspaper! cries B——
Or read only a little at a time and
then digest it with your seven stomachs!

Rumi says:
Do not spend too much time
with an unhappy man.

January 1990, the close of the "cold war"

The Eighth and Thirteenth

The Eighth of Shostakovich,
Music about the worst
Horror history offers,
They played on public radio
Again last night. In solitude
I sipped my wine, I drank
That somber symphony
To the vile lees. The composer
Draws out the minor thirds, the brass
Tumbles overhead like virgin logs
Felled from their forest, washing downriver,
And the rivermen at song. Like ravens
Who know when meat is in the offing,
Oboes form a ring. An avalanche
Of iron violins. At Leningrad
During the years of siege
Between bombardment, hunger,
And three subfreezing winters,
Three million dead were born
Out of Christ's bloody side. Like icy
Fetuses. For months
One could not bury them, the earth
And they alike were adamant.
You stacked the dead like sticks until May's mud,
When, of course, there was pestilence.
But the music continues. It has no other choice.
Stalin hated the music and forbade it.
Not patriotic, not Russian, not Soviet.
But the music continues. It has no other choice.
Peer in as far as you like, it stays
Exactly as bleak as now. The composer
Opens his notebook. *Tyrants like to present themselves as*
patrons of the arts. That's a well-known fact. But tyrants
understand nothing about art. Why? Because tyranny is a
perversion and a tyrant is a pervert. He is attracted by the
chance to crush people, to mock them, stepping over
corpses. . . . And so, having satisfied his perverted desires,
the man becomes a leader, and now the perversions continue

because power has to be defended against madmen like
yourself. For even if there are no such enemies, you have
to invent them, because otherwise you can't flex your
muscles completely, you can't oppress the people completely,
making the blood spurt. And without that, what pleasure is
there in power? Very little. The composer
Looks out the door of his dacha, it's April,
He watches farm children at play,
He forgets nothing. For the thirteenth—
I slip its cassette into my car
Radio—they made Kiev's Jews undress
After a march to the suburb,
Shot the hesitant quickly,
Battered some of the lame,
And screamed at everyone.
Valises were taken, would
Not be needed, packed
So abruptly, tied with such
Frayed rope. Soldiers next
Killed a few more. The living ones,
Penises of the men like string,
Breasts of the women bobbling
As at athletics, were told to run
Through a copse, to where
Wet with saliva
The ravine opened her mouth.
Marksmen shot the remainder
Then, there, by the tens of thousands,
Cleverly, so that bodies toppled
In without lugging. An officer
Strode upon the dead,
Shot what stirred.
How it would feel, such uneasy
Footing, even wearing boots
That caressed one's calves, leather
And lambswool, the soles thick rubber,
Such the music's patient inquiry.
What then is the essence of reality?
Of the good? The mind's fuse sputters,
The heart aborts, it smells like wet ashes,

The hands lift to cover their eyes,
Only the music continues. We'll try,
For the first movement,
A full chorus.
The immediate reverse of Beethoven.
An axe between the shoulder blades
Of Herr Wagner. *People knew about Babi Yar*
before Yevtushenko's poem, but they were silent. And when
they read the poem, the silence was broken, Art destroys
silence. I know that many will not agree with me and will
point out other, more noble aims of art. They'll talk about
beauty, grace, and other high qualities. But you won't catch
me with that bait. I'm like Sobakevich in Dead Souls: *you can*
sugarcoat a toad, and I still won't put it in my mouth.

Most of my symphonies are tombstones, said Shostakovich.

All poets are Jews, said Tsvetaeva.

The words *never again*
Clashing against the words
Again and again
—That music.

Somalia

Compared to being burned alive
When they torch your village
Death by starvation is a good death
Compared with being shot
Dying slowly of wounds
Or being beaten
By frenzied young men
This is much better

You experience little pain
You become like dry wood
Though your lips parch
It is not so bad
You simply shrink up, except for your eyes
Which grow ever larger, like sponges
Taking in the beautiful liquid sun

And the night stars—

And if you are a baby, like me,
Sighing and growing sleepy
Strapped to this woman who keeps
Humming high in her throat
A thing to drive the devil far away
Death by starvation
Is very good, yes, good
As life can be.

October 1992

Saturday Night

Music is most sovereign because more than anything else, rhythm and harmony find their way to the inmost soul and take strongest hold upon it, bringing with them and imparting grace.

—Plato, *The Republic*

The cranes are flying . . .

—Chekhov

And here it comes: around the world,
In Chicago, Petersburg, Tokyo, the dancers
Hit the floor running (the communal dancefloor

Here, there, at intervals, sometimes paved,
Sometimes rotted linoleum awash in beer,
Sometimes a field across which the dancers streak

Like violets across grass, sometimes packed dirt
In a township of corrugated metal roofs)
And what was once prescribed ritual, the profuse

Strains of premeditated art, is now improvisation,
The desperately new, where to the sine-curved
Yelps and spasms of police sirens outside

The club, a spasmodic feedback ululates
The death and cremation of history,
Until a boy whose hair is purple spikes,

And a girl wearing a skull
That wants to say *I'm cool but I'm in pain,*
Get up and dance together, sort of, age thirteen.

Young allegorists, they'll mime motions
Of shootouts, of tortured ones in basements,
Of cold insinuations before sex

Between enemies, the jubilance of the criminal.
The girl tosses her head and dances
The shoplifter's meanness and self-betrayal

For a pair of stockings, a scarf, a perfume,
The boy dances stealing the truck,
Shooting his father.

The point is to become a flying viper,
A diving vulva, the great point
Is experiment, like pollen flinging itself

Into far other habitats, or seed
That travels a migrant bird's gut
To be shit overseas.

The creatures gamble on the whirl of life
And every adolescent body hot
Enough to sweat it out on the dancefloor

Is a laboratory: maybe this lipstick, these boots,
These jeans, these earrings, maybe if I flip
My hair and vibrate my pelvis

Exactly synched to the band's wildfire noise
That imitates history's catastrophe
Nuke for nuke, maybe I'll survive,

Maybe we'll all survive. . . .

At the intersection of poverty and pestilence
The planet's children, brave as hell, juiced
Out of their gourds, invent the sacred dance.

Disco

Another view of the hot young dancers—
Have you seen a baby worm in the dirt
Curl and uncurl like a vibrating spring

When the ants attack it,
Or a cricket after the spider
Hogties its legs

Try to bite and chew its way
Free of the web? The victims
Are so large, their murderers

So little, it must be a dance
Not only of pain
But of incomprehension.

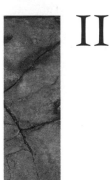

II

The Book of Life

for Sheila Solomon

i

Everything very hardy.
Irises one surprise after another—the florist
Gave me the bulbs cheap, he didn't know their colors,
Big lavender with ruffly Victorian edges,
Pansies, then pinks, gaillardias, yellow with maroon edges and
Maroon centers, all perennials.

Then marigolds orange and gold, and alyssum.
Then I transplanted the beach rose, one of a pair
I bought for Cynthia, so healthy it was breaking the pot—

A blazing fall. The Days of Awe. A Book
Lies open on God's knee, God's ear
Is funneling repentances, but we
Are not in synagogue. Instead we stroll
Through mud around the pool you have bulldozed
In the bright wilderness of your back yard.
Gripping a trowel, you promise me you will swim
Daily. You will draw. You will take long
Walks by the bay.

This is the year your mother finally
Went blind, stamping and screaming *I can see*
Perfectly well and *This is your fault*
While you wept and telephoned nurses and lawyers.
It is the year your favorite uncle died,
He who taught you your first Jewish jokes
And called America *hopeless, politicians*
In bed with profiteers—where he came from, if you saw a Jew
Eating a chicken, you knew one of them was sick.
The year your daughter left for Oregon
To escape you, while you cramp over with dread
Of crowded arteries that could
Any time worsen—

Now we are arm in arm, I stroke your hand
Recalling an old photo of our daughters,
Three slippery toddlers in a bathtub.
Nina looks at the camera with the curious
Eyes of a faun, Rebecca smirks, Eve paddles
In the vicinity of her cosy belly
—If we could reach into that picture,
Splash them teasingly, touch their skin—

You say: *I go into my studio*
And can't recognize it.
What is this place, what did I mean to do,
Will I ever work again.

ii

We know the myth of the artist dying young
Consumptive, crazy,
The lyric poet melting back
Like a jack-in-the-pulpit in April woods,
Created by one rain shower,
Destroyed by the beat of the next,
Crying *My name was writ in water.*
We know too the myth of our self-destructiveness
The slide into a needle, the cave of fur,
The singer burned alive like his smashed guitar.
We were raised on it.
These stories must comfort someone.
Yet other artists continue lives of disciplined labor
Invent strategies to defy the failing eyes,
The weakening arm,
Work larger, simpler, more enraged, or more serene.
Writers sometimes grunt into their eighties
Not necessarily growing witless.
Certain women survive
Their erotic petals and pollen, grasp dirt, bite stone
Muttering *I can't go on, I'll go on*
—No knowing which script applies to us.

That it was we who fed the children language,
That the juice and joy of their growth was ours,

That when they suffered it was we who staggered
Defeated by useless unglamorous grief,
We whom responsibility drove mad, years at a shot
Unable to create, taking to our beds,
To our exhausted pills,
That our yearning for them would be ineradicable,
That we would drone around their whiffs of nectar
Even when they scorned us—Jewish mothers—
Everyone knows this familiar plot, but not
The secret premise. Not how it comes out.

iii

To whom shall we pray
O God of life
Inscribe us in the book of life.
The leaves grow amber, golden, brass,
We walk along the bay, sit on the dock,
Watch ripples spread where a mallard lifts,
My pockets heavy as always
With clicking beach stones.

To be a Jew meant food,
A style of irony, a taste for kindness.
Violin tremolos. We used to think so.
We, the never-included, who believed
God meant the promise, *They shall not hurt nor destroy*
In all my holy mountain.
Today women who gather to pray aloud
By the warm stones of the Western Wall
In the holy city of Jerusalem
Have chairs flung at them, curses spit.
They are called whores
By some who call themselves people of God,
People of the book. A prime
Minister ascends to microphones
Through the sharp wailing of the Intifada
To declaim of those whose lives are in his power
They are as grasshoppers to us
If they dare defy us,
Their children's heads dashed against stones.

In Prague when you asked the doorkeeper
At the Old Synagogue for admission
He said, "Ask in Hebrew," and you could not.
He said, "Ask in Yiddish," and you still could not,
And he refused you.
Who is this God who refuses,
What does the book of life want to tell us.

Uphill your house holds sculpture in every room,
Bronze, silver, gifts to the future, a register
Of pain and anger poured into ugly beauty.
The body's loop from clay to clay.
The unearthed, eroded, lunar archives.
Even as a student, when they said, *Sweetheart,*
Figurative sculpture is dead, you set your jaw
To the perfect formal value of stubbornness,
Another tribal urge, like problem solving—
When the problem is too difficult—
Il faut toujours travailler, said Rodin.
A young woman, a dancer, in leotards
Buttocks of bronze solidly planted
On a high stool, gaze bold and fearful.
Your elderly aunt, palms on trousered knees,
Bronze breasts drooping in T-shirt,
Practical, frank, undeluded.
Youth, knees wide apart, testicles
A temptation to a woman's palm.
Pre-adolescent girl in lotus posture
Patina gunmetal gray as we enter the kitchen.
Archaic figured mirrors, moon-women,
Bound women, women in tears, bulblike
Until one climbs as from imprisonment
Or from a pod, her silvered clitoris
A signal of freedom.
Plaques of a face, your own, much magnified,
Whose fist shadows a stare of brutal rudeness.
The daughter and her girlfriend, caught
Forever in their insolent teens
Are like opened irises.
Hammered metal hair streams down their backs.
The scientist, your husband's colleague

Whom you admire, shambling hands in pockets,
Face blent intelligence and mischief,
Figure an equivalent of his Yorkshire burr.
A bust of our dead friend, bald as she became,
Which it hurt you so much to complete.

In the studio eight feet tall
A goddess still in plaster
Begins at the cleft, ascends through belly, breasts,
To a face again your own, yet strangely calm.
There will be three of this one,
Each a pillar. *Doth not wisdom cry? and understanding*
Put forth her voice? After that, three flying women
Like branches of one tree
Gathered by wind,
Sketched already on the armature.
Can't work? Too afraid,
Tired, guilty?
She is a tree of life to them that lay hold of her
For wisdom is better than rubies.
                                    If the task
As time flies is to press the spirit forth
Unrepentant, struggling to praise
Our hopeless bodies, our hopeless world,
What is required? What pools of luck?
Inscribe us in the book of life.
Perhaps we already know
Where to direct such a prayer.

iv
You started the eight-foot goddess
The year Cynthia spent dying,
The same year you were sculpting
Her small bald head
Fretting you couldn't get
The form. Like all your portraits
It was a compound of yourself and her.
Your zinnias hold out longer than anyone's.
You've planted them where
Extra sun seems to collect
A golden pool near your back kitchen stair.

v

When we think, not of death
But of the decay before it—before us—
I ask you at high noon, who doesn't flinch?
What if there is a season for everything?
Autumn mornings I hear my brain cells pop
One by one, emitting gentle sighs
Like the bubbles in plastic wrapping.
I conjure the stroke, the aphasia,
The nursing home wheelchairs they'll strap me to,
All of me smooth and numb as scar tissue,
The tubes invading my essential holes.
They call me sweet buttercup, dear little buttercup,
I sang that once in *Pinafore*. But a vegetable?
A wilted lettuce?
Or even some crooked wisp
Taken for her daily walk
By a strong brown woman on eraser shoes
—And suddenly you turn and say to me
Whoever we are, we'll be to the end.

Like our friend who died, having decided
No more chemo, no heroic measures.
Lingering? Fuck that, she said.
Morphine for the pain, against the pain.
That final day, her daughters assembled
As she slept and woke, slept and moaned.
They made the decision to switch
To the intravenous. It was morphine all the way then.
All night they waked and watched her sleep
And said from time to time, as she almost surfaced,
She'd sing a line from one of the folk songs
On her Elektra records, that she recorded
When they were kids
And she was almost famous,
As if to sing herself back to sleep,
Then sank again, rose and sank.

Both of us can still reproduce
The downward inflection with which Cynthia would say
In her vibrant near-baritone voice
Sheeeeeit, or Fuuuuck.
We remember her tallness of stature,
Elegant costumes—I coveted in particular
A pair of butter-soft, cherry red
Italian gloves.
We recall her tragicomic love affairs,
Her taste in flowers, Catalan cooking,
Shelves of tattered blues and flamenco records.
She used to describe the folk music scene in America
—*Before money made a hole in it*
And the joy spilled out.
Integrity unobscured by death

Is what we hope for, then.
But to whom should we say
Inscribe me in the book of life.

To whom if not each other
To whom if not our damaged children
To whom if not our piteous ancestors
To whom if not the lovely ugly forms
We have created,
The forms we wish to coax
From the clay of nonexistence—
However persistent the voice
That rasps *hopeless,* that claims
Your fault, your fault—
As if outside the synagogue we stood
On holier ground in a perennial garden
Jews like ourselves have just begun to plant.

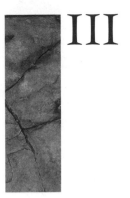

III

Neoplatonic Riff

May, and after a rainy spring
We walk streets gallant with rhododendrons.

When we notice flowers bursting like this
We long to take action too, to fly apart

Like shrapnel, or to stumble up their cones,
Alp after alp overhead, crest above sheerer crest,

Or cram extravagant armloads of petals
Into our mouths and eyes, raspberry ice,

Or press our bodies some way into them,
Even our chests, our bony stiffened legs

That feel suddenly lighter, happier
And more pliant.

We'd let their cold tongues swallow us, recall
A time when we ourselves used to be flowers,

And being in love is similar, in that
It seems to dwell in memory,

That tangled, uncontrolled environment
But behind it, the world of forms—

As when one says, *Don't I know you from somewhere?*
Didn't I used to be you?

After Illness

O lente, lente, currite noctis equi—

i

I picked the books to come along with me
On this retreat at the last moment,
Flinging them into a carton almost randomly,

Not for their greatness, or for any special direction,
So I do have Rumi, Hass, Roethke, Rich,
Olds, Oliver, and the Jew Goldbarth,

But I don't have Rilke or Williams,
And I have a book on Plato a friend gave me,
And the second edition of *The Selfish Gene*

Which I hope will be difficult
And put some bristle in my brains,
But nothing else philosophical

And nobody else's treasure
Or latest fashion. Yes, I have
Some old notebooks of my own

To sieve through, to interrogate,
To make me feel ashamed. For who am I?
Is it possible I still don't know?

What is a dance without some mad randomness
Making it up? Look, getting sick
Was like being born,

They singled you out from among the others
With whom you were innocently twirling,
Doing a samba across the cumulonimbus,

They said *you*, they said *now*,

You had no opportunity to choose
This body or that, as you expected—
At the turnstile, somebody knocked you cold,

It was so unfair.

ii

You woke up thinking it wasn't fair,
But by then it was too late, of course,
You were already glued inside the body

You still possess, or that possesses you,
These rusty chains of being—listen hard,
If the world is rushing

Through a starless, moonless night,
You hear the engine thud, the hiss of water,
You limp through the humid black

To a railing: there,
You can see lights flowing
From a lower deck

Dimly illuminating the
Dizzy white foam, and
You're so alone, but you hear music too,

So you bravely resolve to explore the ship,
And after all, what choice do you have,
And after a few years

You discover they are all
On the same ship, oh yes,
All your friends, your cohorts,

Everyone from before, in their new
Flesh and bones, you agree it's wonderful—
No cause now to be melancholy. Reading? Dancing?

Get up, stand up, thumb some folly
Without which there's no wisdom, you have to
Trust that, you have to take a chance.

Damn choreography. After thirty-six battements
And one tour jeté
Too many, you fall through the trapdoor anyway.

iii
Slowly, slowly—yes, that's what I want
Right now, just that sensation
Of my mind's gradual

Deceleration, as if I
Took my foot off the gas
And the Buick rolled to a stop.

Shadows lucidly
Flutter on the tree trunks
At the wood's edge where I spread

My blanket, wordless—
Hush. Slower, you eighteen-wheelers
On the brain's interstate highways, you eels

In the neural nets, you sharp
Dealers on the trading floor
Of rhetorics, hold your horses, easy there.

Let someone else speak for a change—
My presences,
My guides—

Look at the kids in the cloakroom throwing galoshes
While the teacher tries to introduce
A visitor, a foreign child who waits

With downcast eyes, lashes like brown feathers
On his flushed silk cheeks.
What does my inner mind have on its mind?

If I say, *I'll use this solitude*
To discover my true feeling about my mastectomy,
To do the mourning I've been postponing,

Or if I think, *I'll surrender myself*
To the adoration I feel for X,
Which I prudently control when he's nearby,

Then that's not it!
Whatever I can consciously intend
By definition isn't it!

Hush. Quiet the mind. Leap motionless.
The Tao that can be spoken
Is not the true Tao.

Perhaps I must surrender
The need to write, to metabolize experience
Into poems. Come on, my guides,

Presences, do you think that's impossible?
Do you think it is desirable?
I'm not going to decide this by myself.

Look, I'm just going to turn
Over on my back, on the blanket, nothing
Between here and the sky,

What I want
Is to listen, what I want
Is to follow instructions.

Middle-Aged Woman at a Pond

The first of June, grasses already tall
In which I lie with a book. All afternoon a cardinal
Has thrown the darts of his song.

One lozenge of sun remains on the pond,
The high crowns of the beeches have been transformed
By a stinging honey. *Tell me,* I think.

Frogspawn floats in its translucent sacs.
Tadpoles rehearse their crawls.
Here come the blackflies now,

And now the peepers. This is the nectar
In the bottom of the cup,
This blissfulness in which I strip and dive.

Let my questions stand unsolved
Like trees around a pond. Water's cold lick
Is a response. I swim across the ring of it.

The Figure of Metaphor

for J.P.O., and for Frederick Tibbetts

What a trip, the morning I first saw it
Printed on sides of vans in downtown Athens,
METAPHOROS. Invented here, a local product
Like olives and octopus, what cannot

Be taught, says Aristotle, what genius
Has to discover, the world's uncanny oneness.
In unlike lands it patches parts together,
Bears its own future fruit, a pregnant mother,

Demonstrates when we mount Acropolis
Up footsore steps, jostled and shoved by more
Hasty sightseers, its deep antiquity—
Pericles built these piles to Athens' glory,

Her gleam, so that her democratic harbor
Might welcome tourists from all Asia Minor
Afloat with awe and obols. The idea
Flew; the town boomed as a cultural center,

Meaning a place where one robs foreigners;
Where, conquered by force of arms, one may
Instruct the vulgar victor to surrender
His brutish manners, and by arts and letters

Perceive the gods as motive's metaphors . . .
Today, though they've removed the caryatids,
Blurred by exhaust, like Persephone
Doing her fade-out through mud's molecules,

Poseidon greets the viewer with an arm
Unimpeachably awesome, a mature
Male torso, an unconquerable gaze
Designed to make Odysseus look both ways

Before a crossing—Ocean as a man
I study carefully all afternoon
From every gorgeous storm-reflecting angle
Until ejected by museum guards. Then

Snack: calamari succulent as Eros' thumb,
The feta salad peppery as Zeus,
The retsina fragrant as Boethian woodlands,
Pan's hard and horny hoof. Cordial to come.

Later we amble a boulevard of bars
To a park for *Lysistrata*, history's
First, funniest feminist play, in ancient
Greek, of which I catch one word in ten.

Broomsticks poke from under the men's chitons,
The women wiggle, they too crave the thing
They've been withholding from their warrior
Husbands and boyfriends for a war's duration.

Boldly they shout down from the citadel
Just captured, Hey, Athenians and Spartans,
Forget your martial arts and sign this treaty,
Or else no nooky. While the soldiers sulk,

The women win. Finale, twilight wanes
In the bushy park, the cast begins a folk dance
Waving white wooden doves on poles, sedately,
Then freely, madly; the metaphor remains

Not war but you-know-what. How did they let
Aristophanes get away with that?
Perhaps the town was truly civilized
In ways that Matthew Arnold never got.

What's sweetness and light? Now moth wings dive
For streetlamps as we make for our hotel,
As up the boulevard a vehicle
Stamped METAPHOROS beeps at us; we wave;

As from each jukebox tenors croon of love.

Lockout

He sets his Campus Security cap on the stairs.
I like his mustache and stubby build.
On the third try his master key
Works on my office lock. September 1,
New Jersey tropical, we sit and chat,

Sighing. —I came here when I was five.
Sure, the islands are nice, very nice,
But you can't make money.
I need to improve my vocabulary, he says,
My English. You don't do tutoring?

I don't know about this language lab,
I think I'm blocked. I went to a psychologist,
She said I was blocked.
So how can I advance my career?
I did fine in school in math, science, history,

But never English. Why? Because, when I was small,
They hit my hands with rulers and made me eat soap
For speaking my own language, Spanish.
They punished me and treated me like a foreigner,
And you know what? This is *my* country. When Columbus came,

It was *my* people who greeted him, who said: *Ola.*
We were here before you Anglos, he says,
Resuming his cap, pocketing the master keys.

The Nature of Beauty

I can only say, there *we have been; but I cannot say where.*

—T. S. Eliot

As sometimes whiteness forms in a clear sky
To represent the breezy, temporary
Nature of beauty,
Early in semester they started it.
Lisa read in her rich New Jersey accent,
Which mixes turnpike asphalt with fast food,
A sexy poem that mentioned "the place
Where lovers go to when their eyes are closed
And their lips smiling." Other students grinned,
Thinking perhaps of the backseats of Hondas.
Instead of explaining "place" as a figure of speech,
The teacher wanted them to crystallize
Around it as around the seed of a cloud.
You all understand that? You understand?
The place we go to? Where we've been? They got it.

All semester they brought it back
A piece at a time, like the limbs of Osiris.
Mostly from sex, for they were all American
Nineteen to twenty-one year olds
Without a lot of complicated notions.
But Doug got it from the Jersey shore,
Foam stroking his shins, his need
Leaping in fish form. Robin
One time from dancing
With a woman she didn't
Have sex with, once from her grandmother
Doing the crossword puzzle in pen.
Kindly David from a monstrous orange bus
Whose driver amazed him by kindliness
To passengers who were poor and demented.
Dylan from a Baptist church when song
Blent him into its congregation, sucked him
Into God, for a sanctified quarter hour,

"There's no separation at that height,"
Before it dropped him like Leda back to earth
And the perplexity of being white.

The vapor of the word collects,
Becomes cloud, pours itself out,
Almost before you think: the small
Rain down can rain.
A brief raid on the inarticulate
Is what we get, and in retreat we cannot
Tell where we've really been, much less remain.

The Class

We say things in this class. Like why it hurts.
But what they say outside of class is different; worse.
The teacher hears tales from the combat zone
Where the children live, conscripted at birth,
In dynamited houses. Like all draftees,
They have one job, survival,
And permit themselves some jokes.
Like my father hits the bottle . . .
And my mother. In my office a sofa,
Books, prints, disorder on the desk.
Everything paid for, chosen, they know that.
I've put myself in a drug rehab program
Or *I know I'm anorexic* or *The sonofabitch*
Was raping me for years and now
I'm so frightened for my little sister
But she refuses to talk to me.
Their nervous eyes glide over printed poems
I hand them, but nothing exactly sticks—
The black student pulled apart by his loyalties
Whose bravado breaks like a shoelace
At a cleaning man's curse, *you fuckin' Oreo.*
The homosexual drummer tapping out
A knee tune, wagging his Groucho brows.
Hey, you ought to meet my mom real soon.
'Cause when I tell her, she's gonna die.
Abuse, attempted suicide, incest,
Craziness, these are common stories,
This is street-to-street fighting
Yet these children are privileged.
They're eating.
They have their own beds, and they go to college.

The teacher's job is to give them permission
To gather pain into language, to insist
The critics are wrong, the other professors are wrong
Who describe an art divisible from dirt,
From rotten life. *You have to,*
Of course, you have to write it. What the hell

Do you think Emily did, Walt did, Hart did,
Bill did, Sylvia did. Write for your own sake,
Write for the sake of the silenced,
Write what makes you afraid to write.
The teacher hates the job. She'd like to make
The classroom a stopping-place in a pilgrimage,
Poetry itself a safe-house
Between slavery and freedom.
Since that is impossible,
Since "freedom" is another word
Like "foot" and "ankle" to the amputee,
The teacher helps them descend to hell,
Where she cannot reach them, where books are ashes,
Where language is hieroglyphs carved in walls
Running with slime, which they'll have to feel for
In the steamy mist, while the whip opens their backs.
They'll write about that, or nothing.
Against evidence, the teacher believes
Poetry heals, or redeems suffering,
If we can enter its house of judgment.
Perhaps it is not the poet who is healed,
But someone else, years later.
The teacher tells herself that truth is powerful.
Great is truth and mighty above all things,
Though she would never say so in a class.

Frowning at Emily

The entire room was frowning at Emily
They wanted to know if she was crazy or what
It disturbed them she wrote so many poems
About death madness suffering,
Like: a normal person wouldn't do that,
Would they,
But they were too polite to complain, so
I had to make a speech about it.
Said: you know there are two basic
Approaches to life, some of us try to protect ourselves
Hoping no harm will happen to us
We try for damage control
We cover our rear ends don't we
While others want to experience everything
And are prepared to take the
Consequences—I was making this up
And just one kid in the room
Grinned and exclaimed "cool"
Under his breath.
Of course he was the boy
Who'd had four years of Latin
In high school and loved Virgil
But hell, we're grateful for whatever comes,
Aren't we.

The Vocabulary of Joy

I'm on the grass in front of the library, writing
In the usual notebook.
A couple passes:

Mother African, father Caucasian.
Father to shoulders hoists
Their slender redhead daughter, who

Laughs and shouts, pulling his hair,
You're fun, Daddy, then reaches
A free hand to the mother's

Hand—good enough—except I can't
Describe the laugh. *Barreling*
Doesn't, neither does *pealing.*

Much less can I define the happiness,
Though surely you know what I mean
In the late twentieth century

When I say this.

Locker Room Conversation

There are some men my husband never sees
With their pants on, though they work at the same
University, guys from other departments.
Men, it seems, don't bother wearing towels
In the locker room; though at his age there's often
Plenty to hide, he and his buddies have eyed each other
For so many years, on and off the squash court,
What would be the point? In the shower they chat
About their games, about the last op-ed,
Or they gossip and tell jokes and do business.
He likes to describe this camaraderie
And I like to imagine the naked men
In their various stages of beauty and decay
Splashing, surrounded by brightly falling water—
The muscular definition of smooth youth,
The humorous pouchiness of the middle-aged,
The crisp ligaments of the old, that squashy layer
Of boy-fat under the skin at last consumed,
Their bodies like engravings you could title
"Persistence" or "Integrity,"
And sometimes even the very old,
Softened again like very old wool,
All showering in a hum of conversation.

He likes to mention some of the specimens
I would enjoy—the big-necked boy athletes,
The Indian M.D. in his fifties, graceful as Shiva.
Today he tells me someone he's never seen
Walked into the shower, a kid, near seven feet,
Black curly hair, bronze, except for a bikini mark,
Blue eyes, face of an angel, body of a Greek hero,
Thighs the circumference of my husband's waist,
Dong of a god; and conversation stopped.
Every man just soaped and rinsed himself.
Afterward, as they dressed, my husband asked
A couple of friends. —What did you think of that guy?
—What guy, they said.

Jonah's Gourd Vine

Outside Papyrus Books, Upper Broadway,
The street person in faded sweatpants,
A crackled bomber jacket and missing teeth,
Big handsome man the color of ripe
Aubergines, having laid down a khaki
Parka at the angle of the building,
Admonishes his dog. Sit! Don't sit on the sidewalk!
You'll catch cold! Sit! Sit on the raincoat.
Passersby notice how he's dressed the dog
In a frayed sweater, everyone thinks it's
Heartwarming. Minutes later, though,
I'm inside the bookstore, and he's staggering,
Roaring something quite other, angrily
Over and over up and down the street,
Threats, imprecations, curses it sounds like,
As if the world were coming to an end
And he wanted his voice to bring it down,
So that the girl at the cash register
Murmurs to the assistant in the shop
—That one, I mean it, he's really obnoxious.
Jangles her bracelets and rolls her eyes.
—*Es muy loco,* agrees the other. They make
Red Puerto Rican downturned mouths, while I
Pay for my copy of Zora Neale Hurston's
Jonah novel, thinking how we're all
Here in Nineveh, that great wicked town,
But no sign yet we're ready to repent.

Berkeley: Youth and Age

Winter cabbages blooming in pots
In front of banks and restaurants,
The fashion in Berkeley, it's just like New York,
The world grows smaller and more reassuring,
All this purple and green leafiness
To supplement brokers and panhandlers,
Or do I merely mean more ornamental
While far less reassuring? Now I watch
The delivery man from the bakery van
Flirt with a fellow at the corner table
of the Caffé Strada, once the Mediterranean.
—Hey, weren't you going to talk to me?
—Sure, I thought you were delivering.
The van man sports a torn sweatshirt, gray
Dirt on his cheekbone, a graying Errol Flynn
Mustache, and witty mannerisms
Half homoerotic, half old jock.
The grad student, with chiseled cleancut Frank Merriwell
Features and a massive Saint Bernard
Solid and calm as library paneling
Strolling remotely among the tables,
Is wealthier and younger, therefore used
To being the object of resentful flirtation
To which he responds with good manners
As he was bred; including a slight edge.
Younger man—You've kept your weight down.
Older man—I'm still the stud I was.
Hey, is that your dog?
(Said intermittently with a variety
of inflections. —Hey, is that your *dog?*
Hey, is that *your* dog? Is *that* your dog?)
Youth slips a glance of amused resignation
Across the round table at his companion,
Another clean youngster, who just at present
Is concentrating on his croissant and napkin.
The van man grins to show his canine teeth
And try another cadence.
—Buddy, can I *buy* your *dog?*

After the Reunion

We kept our collars up against the chill,
Embracing, and he said, I love you still,
Before driving away, back to his life,
His home, his three sons, his good wife.
We kissed good-bye. I said, *I still love you.*
Not that I lied, but it was not quite true.

There is a heavenly youth of twenty-one
Inside this kind, suburban gentleman,
The incandescence of whose eyes and mouth
I partially recall. He's driving south,
Humming and smoking Lucky Strikes as if
Kerouac and John Keats composed in him
A solemn brotherhood. It is July,
The radio stays tuned to mariachi
Music the burnt way down from Mexico
City to Acapulco. He's going to
Rent a flamingo pink, baking hot room,
Showerless, with a fly-specked polychrome
Virgin of Guadalupe and a mattress
As thin as a tortilla. There we will press
To give each other our virginity,
And I will not believe my luck, his beauty
And gaiety, the unfathomable way
He throws his curly head backward to laugh
When I pull off my shirt. Outside the town,
Behind a cornfield where we've stolen
A farmer's fresh corn and are feeling good
And wicked, he will find a sandy cove,
Ready to teach me how to bodysurf
Notwithstanding my clumsy unathletic
Body. A miracle! And when I stumble
Victoriously from the foam
After one Andean obsidian wave
Raises and ferries me, I feel I have
Seen through its sunlit spray the suntanned hand

Of San Bartolomeo, on the sand
Waving congratulations. *Great! Terrific!*
As if romance were divine energy—
And so the summer swims, day after day
Thirty years past, then rinses clear away.

ii

Does love move mountains? No, but something does,
And never as we wish, but as time flows.
Time grinds them small, silts up their streams and lakes,
Takes random walks, shuffling its dirty decks.
Time's arrow flies, the least relenting thing
In the known universe. Compelled to string
Along for dear life, do we consent to bless
The ruthless, unimaginable force
Sustaining it, defeating us
Each time we deviate toward timelessness?
In the beginning was the word, the joy
Of an almighty *fiat lux,* the big
Matter-dispersing bang. Since then,
Despite unsystematic moments when
Some bits of dust or flesh cling and cohere,
Entropy moves the sun, the other stars,
Women and men;
Inside a man of fifty there's a boy
I love, and I shall never see again.

Translation

for Judith Hemschemeyer

Pelicans with the nine-foot wingspans
That you say they have
Fly over us while we eat our baskets
Of fried clams and potatoes at the ocean's
Teeming edge among the other tourists.
Across the bay at Cape Canaveral
Some engineers are building something
Stronger and better than the best
Of birds, something
Colossal, but you are describing
Akhmatova, her talons in your chest,
And the way she used to call her poems swallows.
How dare they diminish her fierceness,
You rail at other translators.
A hot breeze brings a chirpy waitress, but
We don't want beer, we're drunk on hazy sunlight,
The billion broken fluted shells
Baked into concrete, a feather
Blown across sand.

The Glassblower's Breath

No point repeating what's already known.
Looking like a grownup, but still
Crayoning in the outlines, a good child,
A good committee member.
Damn, here I am in my fifties
Riding this dumpy bus, that's going nowhere
But back and forth on the same superhighway
With its periodic well-lit tollbooths,
Its refineries, or silos, or satellite disks,
Its passengers all so exhausted yet so determined.

Break the glass, fall toward the glassblower's breath,
That Sufi sentence, it sounds right. I wonder
How to apply it. Should I spring
Into action as we pull around
Some Midwest riverbend whose tame meander
Merely accentuates the land's flatness
For the twentieth time, and say what I'm thinking?
Driver, stop the bus! I'm jumping off!
Don't tell me what city we're coming to
Or if I've left my jacket on the seat,
My belongings in its pockets!
Is it marshland over there?
I can almost hear the frogs
At their mellow nocturnal cantata.
I'm ready to find a pool
In which a harvest moon tenderly bathes.
Its orange soreness urges me to run
Through goldenrod, through ferns, and finally
Into reeds. Into wet.
A stone in the mud
Expects me.
I'll break the moon's face with a single throw.

That is one fantasy. In another
I stay on the bus, night falling and snow
Falling thick and fast over the land,

Skimming the roadway. The lights inside
Go dim, the heater whirs, it's like a home
Away from home, so I begin to sing
In the recessive shower of the skull
Some of the Union songs my dad taught me
When he was that idealist in workshirts
My mother and I would sing along with
Around the oilcloth-covered kitchen table,
While one of us would mash the tuna fish
Into the chopped onions and mayonnaise
For sandwiches he'd take to the meeting.
Which side are you on, we used to shout.
There once was a Union maid, Who never was afraid,
Of goons and ginks and company finks.
Didn't our country used to be different?
Wasn't I once that fearless Marxist kid?
Now the bus labors up
Into the Rockies.
An hour from the Continental Divide
Snow drifts lazily between cliffs,
The owl's fiery eyes beam from his ledge,
Infrared spotlight stroking our carapace,
No meat there . . . *Solidarity forever . . .*
My fellow passengers stir, they awaken,
Tears stand in their eyes like Santas
Ringing their bells on cold street corners.
A child pulls her thumb from her mouth
Popping it like a cork.
A Mexican man flashes a golden tooth.
They all agree to learn these lefty songs.
Everyone joins in, even the driver.

Spoon

for my stepfather

A child in his high chair when the spoon approaches
Widens his mouth to take whatever comes.
Suppose we say it's applesauce. He sniffs,
Tastes and mouths the texture, swallows it.
Tongue flexed and lips compressed
Smooth the receding spoon like a great key
Pulled from a lock, and everyone is pleased
Because the molecules that form a life
Are stacking up. But if it's creamed spinach,
The child rejects the spoon, purses his lips
To seal the entry, sticks the pink tongue out
To poke the spoon away, an act of will
That is an active won't: *I will not—I—*
So begins anyone's tale.

Meanwhile down the street, as tales have ends,
The old man in the nursing home also,
Strapped to his wheelchair, medicated to
A state of presumed calm, and wheeled to where
TV's blue-lit disorienting stare
Immobilizes all the common room,
Retains a will which he can still express.
When the spoon comes, he turns his head sharply
Away, and frowns to show his meaning:
Tightens his lips, then kicks at the spoon's
Bowl with his tongue, as if we're at a soccer
Match, where he's the goalie.

Eighty-six years ago this very mouth
Searched for its ration, open as a bird's.
The head blindly batted a woman's breast—
A head toothless and bald as now, its warm
Scalp stretched over bone—
Thin fingernails that grew so fast
She could hardly keep them shapely cut,
Scratched her flesh while he rooted.
Eighty-six years ago a woman's arm

Circled his arching body, and her thumb
Guided the dripping nipple to his lips.
Touched, he sucked, dragging the bolus deeper,
The strenuous tongue clicked at the back of his palate,
Then the milk came and he shut
His eyes and drank.

My distressed mother tries to force the spoon
Inside this man's mouth, which defeats her plan.
She urges, wheedles, shouts at him, while he
Is rigid as the bedrock of Manhattan,
The only place he ever felt at home
On the range, as he used to joke. Why did they bring him
To these goddamned suburbs? But he stopped asking
That question weeks ago. When my mom visits,
He knows her sometimes and says *Here's my dear wife*
In a mumble nobody can interpret
Except herself, and drools onto the new
Mickey Mouse sweatshirt they have put on him.
But eat is what he won't; instead he rolls
The marbles of his cataracted eyes
At her as if in malice. It is the story
Of the man's life boiled down again to self's
Elemental utterance, *I will not—I—*
Itself a kind of sauce, or humble gravy,
The last before they take the food away,
Resolve to start his tube feeding next day,
Flick off the TV in the common room
And self and utterance alike are gone.

Extraterrestrial: A Wedding Poem for Nina and John, January 2, 1989

Do the angels really
reabsorb only the radiance that streamed out from themselves, or
sometimes, as if by an oversight, is there a trace
of our essence in it as well?

Rilke, *Second Duino Elegy*

Nina and John: there are spaceships circling above us
This afternoon in the raw of winter, the early
Dawn of a new year.

There are extraterrestrial visitors thoughtfully watching
Our cerulean globe spin through its void. As they monitor
Our minor destinies,

If they are able to shiver they do so, hugging
Their bodies, if they have bodies. To them we seem
Perfectly lovely,

A blue-green marble such as a boy would be happy
To keep in his pocket. They watch us pursue our orderly
Orbit around the

Local star upon which our lives completely
Depend, they enjoy our cooling and warming, they clap
Their hands to see it

If they have hands—or perhaps they clap their feelers
Or wave their antennae—they find us a charming spectacle,
Comic and tragic.

At times, too, with their expanded senses,
More powerful than our own, with a subtlety able
To register fainter

Signals, but also different *sorts* of signals,
Not only melodious optic, thundering ultraviolet,
Stridulous X-rays—

Their receptors can pick up what William Blake
Used to call "beams of love": those emanations
Emitted by lovers

That lift from the planet, like particles lighter than air,
Or rather, zap from it, waves more potent than lasers
Pulsing their message:

We have formed a unit, people, we're loving each other,
We are doing it now, can you read us, it's
What we were born for.

To our visitors, such signals are like fireflies
On a summer evening, so pretty, and they like to
Sense the gradations.

Pure sex is the basic beat, a fast percussion.
Sex-plus-love a more eloquent flashing, through a richer
Combination of wavelengths.

The most splendid signal of course is that transmitted
By married lovers, for this one is perfect art
Wedded to nature.

It says: *We're loving, we're working at it, it's like*
Ascending Everest, we're playing, it's
Really sensational,

Different from everything else, it overwhelms us,
Seems to be making us stronger, more alive,
But also weaker—

Difficult, dangerous life, we are up to our eyeballs
In it, we'll never stop. And the visitors look at each other—
Nina and John, are you paying careful attention—

Smiling, applauding, the way we do when children
Learning a skill perform some feat that is difficult,
Since learning to love is something

Like learning to walk, or swim, or ride a bicycle,
It's like writing poems, and maybe like writing history,
—Hard, but rewarding.

Go, say the visitors, mentally egging them on.
You're getting it, yes, you've got it, you can do it,
Congratulations.

They add their wishes to ours. Young man, young woman,
All of us wish you joy, in sex, in love,
And tonight in marriage.

I'm calling them visitors, picturing them in spaceships. . . .
Who are they really? Maybe Rilke was right,
Maybe they're angels.

Taylor Lake

Urge and urge and urge,
Always the procreant urge of the world.
Out of the dimness opposite equals advance, always substance and increase,
     always sex,
Always a knit of identity, always distinction, always a breed of life.

—Walt Whitman

Sunning myself
I gaze at the naked bottom
Of a blond child playing in the sandbox
In Herron Park by No Problem Bridge
Whose mother looks Japanese
Her black hair thick as a horse mane
She's dressing the child now
Buckling pink plastic sandals—and I have to smile—

Another of these racial impurities
That please me so deeply
Our father-mother planet
Working to mix us up.

Yesterday we hiked to Taylor Lake—
Jeep road—no other hikers—
Majestic views all along and up at the ridge
Alpine meadows yellow and vermillion
Azure forget-me-nots springing from moss
Along the saddle some snowfield patches
Scat nestled in turf—wish we could see
The deer that made
These humble droppings—
Jerry and Rebecca climb to the peak
I call to their two small figures
Silhouetted against snow and boulders
And listen to the echo, a very clear one
While Eve and Nat relax under a rock
Out of the wind that sweeps the mountaintops
But with a view of the lake, bright sapphire

I leave them to themselves, young lovers
—One dropped from my body, amazing fortune,
With the handsome youth she has chosen—

I meander among wildflowers, deliberately pathless
Try to slide down a snow slope but
It's too wet for a crust
Look all around
Find two rocks to lie between,
Safe from the wind, under the sky
I lie back and give myself
To the sun for some long minutes
No other human now visible to me
No sound but breeze
A few flies, a bumblebee
And the snowmelt loudly trickling

In an hour my husband and daughter
Back from the peak, he's tired, she's still wired
We all sit under the big rock and eat lunch
Sandwiches, oranges, pinyon nuts
Bittersweet chocolate
There must be a mountain euphoria
Like diver's, you want never
To come back from

Hiking down I notice cirrus bluely scalloped
Eve says it looks like cat fur rubbed backward
Further along eyes caught by miniature
Berry-red, berry-size cones clustered on firs
Crowding the trail calling attention to themselves
Like hundreds of bright pudenda
Until we realize: the air is full of pollen!
Clouds of it thick as fog blowing through forest
Enough to dim the tree trunks! And the cottonwoods
Down by the streams letting go their snowfalls of fluff
With the thin seeds like tiny intelligences—
Fly, fly, everywhere the demand of sex
The floral leap toward procreation
A blessing so lucid
It speaks to us animals
Rouses our drowsy loves—we touch some cones
With our fingertips and release sprinkles of pollen

Midafternoon about halfway
Down the trail there's a sunlit stand

Of pine on a steeply angled opposite slope
Gazing across the distance I can feel
Their sober gratitude
Like men discharged from an army
And all their other sides in chilly shadow
As if putting the thought of struggle behind them
And shifting the pack on my shoulders I think it again,
What it is to be husband and wife, the amazing luck, the
Children of our bodies
Alive in the world, walking ahead of us
Finally a sparkle of creek through woods
The composition of ruby fireweed clump
With rose-clay-colored rocks, water
Falling over, splashing white
Among greenery, almost down the mountain.

Resting and sunning today in the park
Rebecca in blue bikini reads Aristophanes
A man missing a hand strikes up
A conversation—he's here with kids in sandbox—
From Texas, a drawl with some pain in it:

Grandma and gramps came here in a covered wagon
From Virginia in 1920, they were farming people
Their folks gave them a check for five hundred dollars
When they left Virginia, to use
For emergencies, and
Grandma still has that check

Living on her ranch in Carbondale

The main changes were in the 1950s
When they put the ski slopes in—
You can bet the ranch is worth something by now
There's five of us grandchildren, and
My brothers, well, they're fighting
Over this land
But me, he says, *I'd rather keep out of it*
I ain't holding my breath.

Aspen, Colorado, June 1989

Still Life: A Glassful of Zinnias on My Daughter's Kitchen Table

i

In the interminable quest for truth
For the facts as perceived
What has to be included—

The zinnias, in the act—I need
To pay attention—tusking rich golden
Petals in layers, rings, the central rows tipped auburn,
Built blossoms whose spiky digits were at that moment releasing
Their clasp of a polleny core which others still clung to,
Ravishing unconscious golden petals,
But what I also saw
Immediately was
The tangle of flabby leaves, that seemed
The green of old and sagging uniforms
Like cloth laundered to a shabby softness
Sorrowful as the inside of my arm
Crowded and in the process
Of dying, perhaps conscious of it too,
But only later, while drawing the whole mass
In pencil in my sketchbook
And so truly paying attention
Did I notice the buds
Their wrapped repeating patterns
Their sullen spheres like fists
With darkened auburn tips
Surrounded, as they opened or were soon to open,
By thin rigorous leaves, sentinels
Guarding a family of royal youngsters,
Only then exactly to understand
What I see in this tangle is all process
All fierce birth maturity decline
Of some zinnias ripped
From a bush
And this is only one
Glassful of zinnias
And this is only one
Soliloquy

So shall I mention my daughter only married
One month ago
Mention flowering up and down the street
In Berkeley January
Mention a gray green-eyed cat
A lemon tree on the corner
Eucalyptus in the hills
Raining their scent

And this is only one soliloquy

ii
What the eye instantly consents to
Language stumbles after
Like some rejected
Clumsy perpetual lover, language
Encouraging himself: maybe this time
She'll go with me, she'll be nice
And sometimes she does and is, she swivels
Like a powdered blonde on the next bar stool
And turns around upon her glorious flanks,
She is kind to him
And he explodes, he's out of his skin
With foolish pleasure—

It never lasts, however!

So in contrast with the intensity of the hard
Buds, pulling themselves open,
And on the other hand the grief
Of the flabby dying leaves, comes the unconscious
Soaring blossoms' thickened glory
—Consciousness driving itself until it yields
Narcosis of full being, the golden blossoms
The petals of unconsciousness, which in turn break down
At the advent of decay
The very cells break down
Into thought, curling,

Gloomily ironic—
The very cells break down, their membranes crushed
And are dragged, as to a prison

Where the condemned
Beg for forgetfulness
Where the guards
Revel in brutality

iii
Table in the middle of the dining room
Clear grain, a stack of magazines, chipped dishes,
The band of sunlight diagonal on the dusty floor,
The thick telephone book, the daughter at school
Having plunged into it, her existence, having begun to swim hard,
The daughter's husband dreamily at work across the bay,
The mother dreaming also, pencil in hand.

A glassful of zinnias on the table.

Berkeley, January 18, 1990

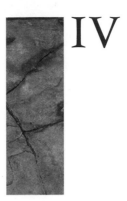

IV

The Mastectomy Poems

1. The Bridge

You never think it will happen to you,
What happens every day to other women.
Then as you sit paging a magazine,
Its beauties lying idly in your lap,
Waiting to be routinely waved good-bye
Until next year, the mammogram technician
Says *Sorry, we need to do this again,*

And you have already become a statistic,
Citizen of a country where the air,
Water, your estrogen, have just saluted
Their target cells, planted their Judas kiss
Inside the Jerusalem of the breast.
*Here on the film what looks like specks of dust
Is calcium deposits.*
Go put your clothes on in a shabby booth
Whose curtain reaches halfway to the floor.
Try saying *fear.* Now feel
Your tongue as it cleaves to the roof of your mouth.

Technicalities over, medical articles read,
Decisions made, the Buick's wheels
Nose across Jersey toward the hospital
As if on monorail. Elizabeth
Exhales her poisons, Newark Airport spreads
Her wings—the planes take off over the marsh—
A husband's hand plays with a ring.

Some snowflakes whip across the lanes of cars
Slowed for the tollbooth, and two smoky gulls
Veer by the steel parabolas.
Given a choice of tunnel or bridge
Into Manhattan, the granite crust
On its black platter of rivers, we prefer
Elevation to depth, vista to crawling.

2. The Gurney

What's this long corridor above the street
What are these glazed beige tiles
Why in my horizontal state
Am I so like an undemanding child

After they wheel me in my bassinet
Into the operating room
Who made the muslin sheets so dry and white
Over my humid body's doom

How radiant the ceiling lights, of course
They buzz appealingly for me alone
I'm special, special, to my Haitian nurse
And now my surgeon pulls rubber gloves on

And now the anesthesiologist
Tells something reassuring to my ear—
And a red moon is stripping to her waist—
How good it is, not to be anywhere

3. Riddle: Post-Op

A-tisket a-tasket
I'm out of my casket
Into my hospital room
With a view of Riverside Drive
Where the snow is a feathery shawl
My children plump as chestnuts by the fire
My son-in-law so humorous and tall
My mate grandly solicitous, a broker
With a millionaire's account.
My friends bob in
And out like apples
Crying and crying *You look wonderful*
While underneath this posh new paisley
Bathrobe that laps me in luxury
Underneath my squares of gauze
I've a secret, I've a riddle
That's not a chestful of medals
Or a jeweled lapel pin
And not the trimly sewn
Breast pocket of a tailored business suit
It doesn't need a hanky
It's not the friendly slit of a zipper
Or a dolphin grin
Or a kind word from the heart
Not a twig from a dogwood tree
Not really a worm
Though you could have fooled me
It was not drawn with crayon
Brushed on with watercolor
Or red ink,
It makes a skinny stripe
That won't come off with soap
A scarlet letter lacking a meaning
Guess what it is
It's nothing

4. Mastectomy

for Alison Estabrook

I shook your hand before I went.
Your nod was brief, your manner confident,
A ship's captain, and there I lay, a chart
Of the bay, no reefs, no shoals.
While I admired your boyish freckles,
Your soft green cotton gown with the oval neck,
The drug sent me away, like the unemployed.
I swam and supped with the fish, while you
Cut carefully in, I mean
I assume you were careful.
They say it took an hour or so.

I liked your freckled face, your honesty
That first visit, when I said
What's my odds on this biopsy
And you didn't mince words,
One out of four it's cancer.
The degree on your wall shrugged slightly.
Your cold window onto Amsterdam
Had seen everything, bums and operas.
A breast surgeon minces something other
Than language.
That's why I picked you to cut me.

Was I succulent? Was I juicy?
Flesh is grass, yet I dreamed you displayed me
In pleated paper like a candied fruit,
I thought you sliced me like green honeydew
Or like a pomegranate full of seeds
Tart as Persephone's, those electric dots
That kept that girl in hell,

Those jelly pips that made her queen of death.
Doctor, you knifed, chopped, and divided it
Like a watermelon's ruby flesh
Flushed a little, serious
About your line of work
Scooped up the risk in the ducts
Scooped up the ducts
Dug out the blubber,
Spooned it off and away, nipple and all.
Eliminated the odds, nipped out
Those almost insignificant cells that might
Or might not have lain dormant forever.

5. What Was Lost

What fed my daughters, my son
Trickles of bliss,
My right guess, my true information,
What my husband sucked on
For decades, so that I thought
Myself safe, I thought love
Protected the breast.
What I admired myself, liking
To leave it naked, what I could
Soap and fondle in its bath, what tasted
The drunken airs of summer like a bear
Pawing a hive, half up a sycamore.
I'd let sun eyeball it, surf and lake water
Reel wildly around it, the perfect fit,
The burst of praise. Lifting my chin
I'd stretch my arms to point it at people,
Show it off when I danced. I believed this pride
Would protect it, it was a kind of joke
Between me and my husband
When he licked off some colostrum
Even a drop or two of bitter milk
He'd say *You're saving for your grandchildren.*

I was doing that, and I was saving
The goodness of it for some crucial need,
The way a woman
Undoes her dress to feed
A stranger, at the end of *The Grapes of Wrath,*
A book my mother read me when I was
Spotty with measles, years before
The breast was born, but I remembered it.
How funny I thought goodness would protect it.
Jug of star fluid, breakable cup—

Someone shoveled your good and bad crumbs
Together into a plastic container
Like wet sand at the beach,
For breast tissue is like silicon.
And I imagined inland orange groves,
Each tree standing afire with solid citrus
Lanterns against the gleaming green,
Ready to be harvested and eaten.

6. December 31

I say this year no different
From any other, so we party, the poets
And physicists arrive bearing
Cheeses, chile, sesame noodles,
Meats, mints, whatever—
Champagne—
Filling up the sideboard,
Filling the house up, filling it.
At midnight everyone kisses,
My man replenishes
His wicked punch,
My mother folk dances,
In the kitchen they pass a joint,
Then after that they put
The hard rock on,
And I, dressed
In black tights and a borrowed
Black and red China silk jacket,
Am that rolling stone, that
Natural woman

No different, no
Different, and by 3 A.M. if
The son of my blood
And the wild student of my affection
Should choose to carry on, if
My goddess daughter with her satiric
Stringbean boyfriend
Tuck themselves into the bunk
Bed of her girlhood, may they hear me
Mutter in sleep, sleep
Well and happy
New year.

7. Wintering

i had expected more than this.
i had not expected to be
an ordinary woman.

—Lucille Clifton

It snows and stops, now it is January,
The houseplants need feeding,
The guests have gone. Today I'm half a boy,
Flat as something innocent, a clean
Plate, just needing a story.
A woman should be able to say
I've become an Amazon,
Warrior woman minus a breast,
The better to shoot arrow
After fierce arrow,
Or else *I am that dancing Shiva*
Carved in the living rock at Elephanta,
One-breasted male deity, but I don't feel
Holy enough or mythic enough.
Taking courage, I told a man *I've resolved*
To be as sexy with one breast
As other people are with two
And he looked away.

Spare me your pity,
Your terror, your condolence.
I'm not your wasting heroine,
Your dying swan. Friend, tragedy
Is a sort of surrender.
Tell me again I'm a model
Of toughness. I eat that up.
I grade papers, I listen to wind,
My husband helps me come, it thaws
A week before semester starts.

Now Schubert plays, and the tenor wheels
Through Heine's lieder. A fifteen-year survivor

Phones: *You know what? You're the same person*
After a mastectomy as before. An idea
That had never occurred to me.
You have a job you like? You have poems to write?
Your marriage is okay? It will stay that way.
The wrinkles are worse. I hate looking in the mirror.
But a missing breast, well, you get used to it.

8. Normal

Assent, and you are sane. . . .
—Emily Dickinson

First classes, the sun is out, the darlings
Troop in, my colleagues
Tell me I look normal. I am normal.
The falsie on my left makes me
In a certain sense more perfectly normal.
An American who lives beyond my means,
A snake-oil foot in the door,
A politician with a strong
Handshake in an election year.
Crafted of latex, it repairs the real.
Like one of those trees with a major limb lopped,
I'm a shade more sublime today than yesterday.
Stormed at with shot and shell,
A symbol of rich experience,
A scheme to outlive you all.

Meanwhile a short piece of cosmic string
Uncoiled from the tenth dimension
Has fastened itself to my chest.
Ominous asp, it burns and stings,
Grimaces to show it has no idea
How it arrived here.
Would prefer to creep off.
Yet it is pink and smooth as gelatin.
It will not bite and can perhaps be tamed.
Want to pet it? It cannot hurt you.
Care to fingertip my silky scar?

Now I am better, charming. I am well.
Yes, I am quite all right. I never say
The thing that is forbidden to say,
Piece of meat, piece of shit.
Cooled, cropped, I'm simple and pure.
Never invite my colleagues
To view it pickled in a Mason jar.

9. Healing

Brilliant—
A day that is less than zero
Icicles fat as legs of deer
Hang in a row from the porch roof
A hand without a mitten
Grabs and breaks one off—
A brandished javelin
Made of sheer
Stolen light
To which the palm sticks
As the shock of cold
Instantly shoots through the arm
To the heart—
I need a language like that,
A recognizable enemy, a clarity—
I do my exercises faithfully,
My other arm lifts,
I apply vitamin E,
White udder cream
To the howl
I make vow after vow.

10. Years of Girlhood (for My Students)

All the years of girlhood we wait for them,
Impatient to catch up, to have the power
Inside our sweaters to replace our mothers.

O full identity, O shape, we figure,
We are God's gift to the world
And the world's gift to God, when we grow breasts,

When the lovers lick them
And bring us there, there, in the fragrant wet,
When the babies nuzzle like bees.

11. The River

Sluiced with the city's detritus
To the glum hands of the sea,
Afraid of dark, afraid of cold,
She turns and calls for me.
When other fragments,
Each a portion gone
Before whoever loved it,
Paddling along beside her
Offer to be friends,
She shies like a spooked horse,
Shivering, whimpering—it's
As if a girl went off
From the safe playground
For a private walk and found
Herself in the wrong neighborhood
—Strange cars, strange businesses,
Too many ugly grown-ups
And none her mom. She knows
There can be no real danger
Yet it is dark, it's cold,
The ebb tide flows so swiftly,
The searching kisses of fish,
The ironic salute of crabs,
The ghostly pallid weeds
Never comfort a person.
Isn't she too big to cry?
Of course, to cry is dumb,
To be brave is smart,
Yet her lip trembles,
Carry me, mama. Sweetheart,
I hear you, I will come.

12. *Epilogue: Nevertheless*

The bookbag on my back, I'm out the door.
Winter turns to spring
The way it does, and I buy dresses.
A year later, it gets to where
When they say *How are you feeling,*
With that anxious look on their faces,
And I start to tell them the latest
About my love life or my kids' love lives,
Or my vacation or my writer's block—
It actually takes me a while
To realize what they have in mind—
I'm fine, I say, *I'm great, I'm clean.*
The bookbag on my back, I have to run.

The author and publisher wish to express their grateful acknowledgment to the following publications in which some of the poems in this collection first appeared, some in earlier versions: *American Poetry Review* ("The Mastectomy Poems," nos. 4, 6, 7, "Still Life: A Glassful of Zinnias on My Daughter's Kitchen Table"); *Antaeus* ("After the Reunion"); *The Atlantic* ("Locker Room Conversation"); *Boulevard* ("The Studio"); *Colorado Review* ("Taylor Lake," "Translation"); *Denver Quarterly* ("Nude Descending"); *5 A.M.* ("Frowning at Emily," "Lockout," "The Vocabulary of Joy"); *Kenyon Review* ("The Mastectomy Poems," nos. 2, 3, 5, 8, 9, 10, 11, 12); *Long Shot* ("In Our Time: A Poem to Aphrodite"); *Missouri Review* ("Boil," "Surfer Days"); *Ms.* ("The Mastectomy Poems," nos. 1, 6); *The Nation* ("Appearance and Reality," "Jonah's Gourd Vine"); *New England Review* ("After Illness"); *Nimrod* ("The Book of Life"); *Ontario Review* ("Alice Before Her Widowhood," "Globule," "Middle-Aged Woman at a Pond," "Triptych"); *Paris Review* ("The Boys, the Broom Handle, the Retarded Girl"); *Poetry* ("The Figure of Metaphor," "The Orange Cat"); *Poetry East* ("The Class"); *Poetry Flash* ("The Eighth and Thirteenth"); *Prairie Schooner* ("The Glassblower's Breath," "The Nature of Beauty," "Neoplatonic Riff," "Spoon"); *Santa Monica Review* ("Migrant," "Revolution as Desire"); *Seneca Review* ("The Death of the Poet," "The Russian Army Goes Into Baku"); *Shenandoah* ("Anecdotes Without Flowers: 1919"); *Triquarterly Review* "At the Van Gogh Museum," "Disco," "Marie at Tea," "Saturday Night"); *Virago Book of Love Poetry by Women* ("Extraterrestrial: A Wedding Poem for Nina and John, January 2, 1989").

"The Eighth and Thirteenth" received the 1994 Anna Rosenberg Award for poems on the Jewish experience.

I wish to express my gratitude to the New Jersey Arts Council, for an award which helped give me time to complete this manuscript.

Alicia Suskin Ostriker is a poet and critic, author of seven previous books of poetry, including *The Imaginary Lover,* which won the 1986 Poetry Society of America William Carlos Williams Award. Her poetry has been widely anthologized and has been translated into French, German, Italian, Japanese, Hebrew, and Arabic. She is also the author of *Stealing the Language: The Emergence of Women's Poetry in America* and *The Nakedness of the Fathers: Biblical Visions and Revisions.* She has received grants from the National Endowment for the Arts, the Rockefeller Foundation, and the Guggenheim Foundation. She lives in Princeton, New Jersey, and is professor of English at Rutgers University.

The Crack in Everything

is typeset in Meridien in QuarkExpress.

It was designed and paged by

Kachergis Book Design

in Pittsboro, North Carolina.

It was printed by

Thomson-Shore, Inc.,

in Dexter, Michigan

Library of Congress Cataloging-in-Publication Data

Ostriker, Alicia.

The crack in everything / by Alicia Ostriker.

p.   cm. —(Pitt poetry series)

ISBN 0–8229–3936–3 (cloth : alk. paper).—

ISBN 0–8229–5593–8 (pb : alk. paper)

I. Title. II. Series.

PS3565.S84C7   1996

811′. 54—dc20   95–43297